SECRET CITIZEN

Also by Arthur Gregor

Poetry:

Octavian Shooting Targets
Declensions of a Refrain
Basic Movements
Figure in the Door
A Bed by the Sea
Selected Poems
The Past Now
Embodiment and Other Poems

For Children:

The Little Elephant *(Photos by Ylla)*
1 2 3 4 5 Verses *(Photos by R. Doisneau)*
Animal Babies *(Photos by Ylla)*

Plays:

Fire!
Continued Departure
The Door Is Open

Memoir:

A Longing in the Land

SECRET CITIZEN

Poems

Arthur Gregor

The Sheep Meadow Press

Riverdale-on-Hudson, New York

Printed in the United States of America
Typeset in ITC New Baskerville by Keystrokes, Lenox, Massachusetts

The Sheep Meadow Press
Riverdale-on-Hudson, N.Y. 10471

Distributed by New Amsterdam Books
171 Madison Avenue
New York, N.Y. 10016

Library of Congress Cataloging-in-Publication Data

Gregor, Arthur, 1923–
    Secret citizen.

    I. Title.
PS3557.R434S44   1989   811'.54   88-32701
ISBN 0-935296-78-6

ACKNOWLEDGMENTS

Some of these poems first appeared in the following periodicals:

HUDSON REVIEW: *In Dark's Cover*
THE SOUTHERN REVIEW: *The Threshold, or, My Home in Winter*
THE NATION: *Old Offense; Mozartian; On Another Departure, Châtillon 1987*
QUARTER MOON: *Spirit's Taunt*
A JUST GOD: *Dianabad, Vienna 1937; Antibes, The Evening Hours*
PIVOT: *Dark Converse*
NEW LETTERS: *Signals* (originally entitled *The Fleeting*)
PRACTICES OF THE WIND: *Outside Gien*
SONORA REVIEW: *77th Street Fair*
INTERIM: *Art Songs, # 2, 5 & 6*
WORLD LITERATURE TODAY: #5 from *The Poem of Heaven Within*
#10 & 13 from *The Poem of Heaven Within* were included in A CELEBRATION FOR
    STANLEY KUNITZ (Sheep Meadow Press, 1986)

Contents

One

To the memory of Jacqueline Rozendaal Harvey

In Dark's Cover

1.

Almost wherever I look in this tree-rimmed
wide river's valley there are reflections,
in canals, those no longer in use covered with
the foliage's bright green refuse, in others
still trafficked by coal-bearing barges black as
their cargo, or by pleasure craft trimmed
with flags, strung-up wash, open beach umbrellas.
There are as well slender streams not deep
but rushing with strength between the fields
they nourish. Cattle come there to drink,
for a long time standing in groups in the
deep shade of trees, enormous whether they
be linden, birches, willows, chestnut, acacias;
no matter which, the darkness they form is
the same, the patches of dark in the water
where the heads of the cattle are mirrored
and where spears of light through the branches
sparkle in the shimmering surface, the same.
Then there are amidst a variety of evergreens—
like other trees here grown to great heights
due to a favored condition of water and light—
and around the stone foundations of once
great homes, still ponds, moat-like, with narrow,
by now barely passable bridges, where float
water-lilies, shiny green leaves and other
flora that flourish in still, dark water.
An occasional magpie or wild duck
fluttering up, skimming the surface in some
pursuit, disturbs the serenity, or adds a
characteristic sound to the stillness
lingering across the ponds like the mist in
the early hours of the day. The feeling around

the ponds is grotto-like, an underwater world
of varying shades of green, creepers wound around
mossy treetrunks, flutterings from often invisible doves
high in the branches like bats in the depth of domes,
chirpings, twitterings sounding from the grotto
stillness, the watery darkness. Whose trills
from where? Whose the branches? the dark, the stillness,
the blotches in the water having wiped away
distinctions, colorations, gender, species...

2.

I wake from a dream, drenched by the dark's immense
cover wherein, waterlike, appearances, events
are altered, the sameness behind a striving,
an urging toward unalterable essence, glimmers
like the light the water captures and transmutes
regardless of the sky's muteness or brightness
into the soul-soothing glow of sameness, of oneness.
A murmur, a rippling ongoingness,
the presence that remains unseen, unperceived,
is not of the nature of diversity, nor of
competitiveness or conflict, has captured me.
No recognizable shapes, nor sounds; only
the dark's soothing infused without sensation.
And the wonder, deep wonder of recognition,
comprehension.
                    I had understood in the dream
that there where I was it was missing;
that violence ruled in its place; that I must
escape dislocation, must make my way back
to where the visage rests, where welcome
remains unchanged. In the fear-ridden street
someone I knew approached me and as though
he had read my thoughts, said: "We are not
separated there. Only here, where going one's own way

is assumed to be the only good, only here
are we enmeshed in turmoil, separateness."
And putting his arm around my shoulder
made me feel that I was once again embraced
as perhaps I had only been in someone's heart.
And thus flowed we on into the dream's immense
cover, the watery darkness covering sightless
indivisible light. I wake. Outside, the great
dark trees stand silent, ancient, unmoved
as time. Of their reflections in the stream
that enters the wide river down below not far
from where I've slept, their trunks, branches,
leaves, lacelike blossoms on the frailest stems;
—of all that makes them trees, nor of the sky,
dark sky between the leaves, nothing can be
discerned in the water—as though the dark,
abolishing distinctions, had blinded it.

The Threshold, or, My Home in Winter

1.

How often, as the years like this snow first melting then
accumulating, have drifted past, have I not had
in dreams knowledge of belonging—being back in
some scene of childhood, a tree-lined, bench-lined
city street, a farmyard, country house and garden,
when the things that rose to intimate awareness
made for what was later, longingly, thought of as
the element of home? some assent-giving Invisible,
almost tangible evidence of the Intangible Near!
Like music that makes real our feelings,
dreams, our lives' storybook aspects, those that
are forecasters of possible fulfillments,
have often made real the reality of home
where a woman you had almost forgotten awaits you,
apparition of feelings, of music, of welcome
mysteriousness waiting on the doorstep to take you
into the secret that lives with her inside.

Yet is this house, the first I can call my own,
this house and garden where I may now belong
to what belongs to me, is this small town,
this continent where grew the music coming to me just now
from another room, on an unaccompanied cello
consolations that are the result of faith and
technique which, combined, can speak for this human need—
fulfillments so natural, so simple,
the arrival at and giving ourselves to
the one imperative none escapes,
the only thing truly familiar—is this, now
my house, my home in winter anything other than
what has always been looked toward, steered toward:
the permanent, the blissful Intangible?

For the spaces, the spaces themselves are lonely,
the mortar, new walls, old beams that support the roof
where once a ladder led, wine-barrels and bales were kept,
and the lives lived there have paled more than
the snow melting off the roof down the stone walls.
And lonely, more than lonely, cold, inhuman,
aloof when left to themselves, when not visited
by women bending to pull weeds or lay flowers,
the crosses and headstones in the snow-coated
cemetery above. An isolated sparrow sits on a wire,
sudden showers of snow are shaken from the evergreen's
dark branches. There is no one coming up the stairs,
though I had turned with a start, thinking someone
was standing there, some memory, some former presence
tongueless, amazed and staring at the changes.

And empty, empty and lonely the spaces outside.
Like a white ocean, the fields under thick snow
stretching toward the horizon and an unambiguous sky
heavy with itself, with thick moisture about to fall.
Two blackbirds screech above the moonlike whiteness.
Across the road, nothing but greyness, wisps of smoke
rising from low houses scattered among the buried fields.
The tangible things, tangible implements
dispersed, forgotten, lonely...
                              A black carriage-frame
on high, thin-rimmed wheels, a decoration now
on someone's lawn, brings to mind flights
across similar scenes, trudgings that left
but flimsy tracks, of peasants driven on
by dire want, of troops of actors dragging
their sceneries, the wigged and powdered women
thrust about in the drafty wagons, the men pushing,
uttering lines long since faded on crumpled pages.
Quests, the crossings of desolate winter spaces,
the flights to known or unknown destinations,
a swarm of birds across a sky threatening, vast and

unremitting...grey, grey the world outside...
the ruts from wheels, footprints of pushing,
muttering men and boys, all by drifts absolved,
wiped out.

       And of the snow-covered city streets,
the skating rink in a park an empress had owned,
a boy's attempts and failures on the ice,
the warm moments inside around a glowing stove,
the smell of wetness and burning coals,
the walk home through the bitter cold:
what of the scenery now, the foyer still frigid
but beyond the tall doors, the warm rooms,
that had described a boy's world in winter?

And of the many other occurrences we remember,
things touched, faces held, what has continued but
the sense, or want, they contained and conveyed, of belonging...?
The moments of reflection, not of features
but of what we extract from them, from the forms,
from the occasion and from those who make up
the occasion, and the place and the season:
extract what is contained in them and is
the same in each, which is what we retain—
remembering the moment of remembrance
in a mirror above a mantle, in an inn
on a winter visit in a New England town.

2.

Streaks in the sky, tracks across roads, flights
of the needy,—and who among us is not so
in this illusory world, the stations blurred,
the things attained inadequate, discarded?
Driven by inherent impoverishment
but also by a sumptuous reality that,

though dimly perceived, has affected each
by hints in words they have now at heart,
in dreams whose unlikely musical events
surround us like silent companions,
actors have moved their sceneries, men
their households on wagons, have had to stop
and shield their eyes when the distances ahead
are suddenly consumed in a winter glare
and all that is far but visible has burst into
invisibleness. They dare not go forward, they cannot
go back. Can they take the only turn they must make
to find themselves where they have craved
to be? Shrouded in luminous nearness
the home that awaits them.

What prevents us
from remaining where, with unbounded tolerance,
her fullness of being that appears to us as
patience, she waits on the threshold at our arrival?

As such this grey world cannot content us on
a winter day. How often have I not listened for
the call of desiring objects, seeking forgetfulness
in bodies, the broader ranges and heightened awareness
only the contact with nearness can give?
The musical descriptions of intimacy with
the sublime! Even now, in this setting,
the possibilities haunt me, if mostly again
in dreams. Bodies together in a glow of sanctity,
luminous oneness in the guise of brother
to brother. But in this actual world
what we take away with us is solacing sorrow.
The scenes we went out to, heeding a common call,
were full with desire, the long steps in sunshine,
the flowery grasses, a solitary figure
looking out on the sea, elbow resting on the wall.
The solace we feel, having taken away with us

the sorrow of their bereavement—for we had asked
of them, had bled them for what they cannot give—
is akin to consolations in music.
                              We are not
at home in things, only in the element of home
giving things their home.

                    Therefore is she
who would let us reside in the secret whose allure
we have longed for, even prayed for
in this seasonal habitat, now the drowse of winter,
she whose bodily opulence and cheer are but
the speech of mysteriousness to which she
would bring us, the utter expansiveness
where are dimly perceived the planes and angles,
shaped harmony of the most solid of structures
soaring and intimate, we have travelled far
to enter, the condition akin to oblivion
we come to when our desires are merged with
desiring objects—body to body, and ahead
through the open doors, the flowery grass
and the pale-colored ocean—
                              therefore, as we come
to her, as she takes us inward, is she as well
sign of our renewed departure. For in arriving
we must also, we must still depart. "You go
to come back" I had heard Him say, from out of the depth,
who is, above all, Immutable Steadiness.

As they alter and fade, as the things of
this world turn vague, stand as though in dreams
at the edge of nothingness, where but in us
is their sorrow, where but in us their home?
Perhaps in death we abandon them, except
that even then some spectre may linger
which a creature with intenser sense may detect
with a screech, long stare, shudder of wings...

10

The long view we have from the bridge of the river,
the surface chopped now as though covered with scales,
the vague smokiness of the winter air, the brownness
of sticks on the ground that once were twigs on trees,
the sky dark and swift: —who will lift this into
the felt sadness it pleads for, to be shared
as one shares closeness with an animal in one's arms?
how, without us, can it be winter's coziness?

O threshold, o blissful Intangible,
o concept contained in the pillar, the lintel,
music whose consolation we have at heart, always:
this time-held, this wintry scene waits for us also.

The precinct that is our home is outside
of time, dimly we perceive the boundaries.
Here, vanishing things hold us, their sorrow
and the solace that comes from the moments,
the songs outside of time that return us to time,
to the wintry season where we trudge onward,
where we also belong, weary but grateful.

For it is here where we rise from dreams of
her homeland, from a return of a brother
to timeless youth, to limbs resonant with spirit.
Here where I wake to the house I've dreamed of
as home, to the trees, tall, bare, not resisting
the winds; to slow wisps of smoke from the house
beyond mine; to the wintry sky in the window,
a sky grey, grim, light-streaked, and unambiguous.

The Poem of Heaven Within

"Transitoriness is everywhere plunging into a profound Being."
—Rainer Maria Rilke

"Attributeless, changeless and unconditioned, I am the abode of Love."
—Sri Atmananda

1.

Even if now daily occurrences occasion little
to startle that part of the being that lies
in wait always, that can be roused only
by indications from that other realm
of which he, that inner part, is secret
citizen; even if now out in the streets
or indoors when among mostly unknown people
little happens to rouse him, as it once did,
and often—between skyscrapers, a brilliant
wintry sky reflected in walls of glass and
steel, a single gull fluttering above the street
as though it had lost its way; a clarity of
celestial harmony, a glow of choral quality
surrounding the extreme metropolis;
or, in foreign places, unexpected glimpses
of a most familiar intimacy, of a way of
being as one once knew and has not forgotten,
come to life again, suddenly, quickly,
by a garden wall, sunstreaked, silent,
only the hum of silence, blossoms, all shades
of flowers tumbling across, a path to
the house, a shape of roof, the appearance
of something contained and total
one dreams of as having remembered in a dream;
and most engaging, most gripping of all
the promise of love in a face not seen

until then but known and remembered always.
Even if sudden appearances of heaven's
hidden life on earth, instants of
illumination, of essence breaking through
the forms that contain it, of shudders
when observing recognition in others,
when someone is astounded by having touched
or been touched by the thing we know best,
for which there is no name but all know
and share, when someone is overcome by
emblems from the realm of perfection,
assurances, greetings in the way one was
looked at, or in the way the sky looked,
an opulence of clouds across an immense
landscape of tended fields and hills;
or when one is oneself startled by
the actual promise of achievable desires
others propose by their perfectly harmonious
physical presence, the containment
of the sublime in their physical forms—
observers brought to the condition of
divine oblivion by perfection that
for the least instant consumes the observed—:
even if these have lost the power
to rouse heaven's aspect in the self,
even if in daily lives such occurrences
are rare, such appearances by now
worn out, they are not so in dreams,
not when the part that is hidden there
dominates and demonstrates his truth.

2.

Is it a dream or is it actually occurring
when a most welcome event takes place?
You are on a stage, the sounds you are
about to sing, words about to form
are fully shaped in you even before
you utter them, possessed as you are
by then by the bliss they mean to convey,
and as you look out into the hall,
at the faces you're about to astonish,
as you are about to start, you wake.
When the miraculous moment which you
and all those come there to hear
have already known, is about to happen,
and the corpse you are looking at
changes in its coffin before you
into the very essence of knowledge,
the very proof of the bliss you
have always been convinced exists
and is now there in the face in front of you—
o miraculous, o most welcome event!
Is the unfolding in a dream of
the one possession that remains with you
even if everything is taken away,
the secret that is left shining
like the white rose you've put before
the face that is now a photograph in your room,
the flower at the height of its flowering:
is the unfolding in a dream of that
which is secret but known any less real
than occurrences you say are real
because you are awake, but do not
remember them, those that take you
from here to there, from one
thing to another, and that is all?

3.

And of those you do remember, events
you do not want to forget, indications
of the harmonious reality that you
have always sought in encounters—
a slow drive in the country above
the wide river's ample valley,
the evening mists lifting in the fields,
the serenity when nature readies itself
for sleep; or again, the face that stands out
in a crowd, a solitary figure waiting
in a setting that suggests nothing but
anticipation—: of those scenes, cherished
events that you remember, is it not
as though they happened as in a dream?
For they are always most welcome, always events
that astonish us because they are foreknown.
And when they occur, occur as though
this event of our remembrance happened there
where time's flavor is altered,
where change, the changes have shed
their shadings, perturbations, demarcations.
Birdsounds, the long light of evening,
low-roofed farmhouses scattered among
the fields, a cyclist coming out of the bushes
pedalling swiftly away on the empty road,
vast, vast the sky, the clouds enormous...

4.

They are not different then, for they
are, dreamed or not, indications of
an ease, a splendor completely achieved,
colors at the height of clarity,
contours of grace and gracefulness,
combined all in a simple stateliness,
simple because natural; call it
a sphere, an elevation, whose calm, order,
arrangement of parks and avenues is unaffected
by the condition you are in, asleep or not,
this source of the imagination,
this stable dominion whereof we feed.
And why but for that have you directed
yourself from early on, from when you
set forth on your dream of youth, heeding nothing but
its cause, and you sought, have sought
them always, the shades of permanence,
the long stone passages whose light, dim,
almost dull, is never altered; have sought
them in the briefest episodes,
fleetingest moments when you glimpsed
bright flowers after the rain, or sat,
forehead to forehead, arms around arms, on the bed.
Why but for that have I been your complement,
the image you had to discern, and when
you did, felt afterward that the identity,
the intimacy was such that it had to have been
the reflection of yourself you had uncovered,
had come close to in this exploring,
this step by step accession and removal
like a boatman who loses the distance he
has gained, the shoreline at last before him:
—events in which, glimpsing the outlines of
your deepest knowledge, you lost
yourself, gaining your loss—events
which, dreamed or not, you remember.

16

5.

And do not call it a dream when he appears
in whom lives nothing but the splendor of
reduction, the awareness no longer perceptible
when everything that comes up before one
has been removed and what is left is the
pure bliss of irreducible being
which issues from him and touches you,
lifts up in you what has lain there dormant
and is the same as what he is only not
awakened until he appears and he tells you
that he has lived with you always,
down the corridor like the lodger of whom
one does not take much notice but who
has come now, and only he knows why now,
to at last declare you to yourself.
And you announce to someone else
who also lives with you, that he has come
at last. And you stand, both of you,
bathed in his bliss, and there is not,
there never has been any other happiness,
for this is the source of whatever it is
that has made you happy. And it is as though
even your flesh dissolved in the water of
this bliss, that even your body has become
insubstantial, nothing but the flow,
this heaven that flows nowhere, that is less
than aqueous, a shine less of a discernible glow
than of the lamps on a bridge in the darkness
below. And in the dream you can hardly believe
that this has in fact happened to you
but know it has, for you have always
known him, but inadequately; and now,
he has come before you, has declared you,
and has removed, for now, this in-
sufficiency. And the day that follows,

the day itself seems washed in the bliss
he had awakened, washed in a clarity
as you have rarely seen, as you sit
on your terrace still dazed by the wonder,
feeling no less afloat than the wind
that sways the poplars in the distance,
the lilies, strung vines and roses nearby,
touches them as though the wind itself
were nothing but a wind of light,
and the brightness is marked by a sharpness,
the darkness of shadows, of clouds, of trees,
of houses, as distinctly dark as
the brightness is bright. And it stays with you,
the effect of the wondrous encounter,
and you know it was not a dream
but the stare of reality itself
that had come to you in dream's guise.

6.

There have been times, there have been places
of a commingling, the stamping upon earth
of contours of the range beyond the range
of time, in obscurest terms
suggestions of a colossal magnificence—
man's burden, his awesome terror—
where the imagination starts,
and there walked, has always walked
one who knew, whose radiance seeped
into the soil for sustenance
and later into works composed
to encase utterances and deeds—
for we, too, are not sustained
unless joined to that of which we are—
whose plain goodwill had spread
like waters of a flood into the sleep
of all. And the voices you hear today,
always high as though in imitation of
the child, or aspiring to reach,
with trumpets as support, the end,
the limit of sound, are at once
from lofty spaces and residual chambers
you have within yourself. And when
you can, you prefer to go for this accord
to where the hymns, modulated as
in supplication by a humble bass,
were sung, and even if the squares
are silent and you hear the water splash
against the stones, the strong sun
casting long and lingering shadows on
the walls, there reverberates each time
within yourself a response to what once
was there, imprints still of what
not time nor denials could erase.

7.

What are your thoughts when on waking
the heavenly voices are vanished,
or you are back to the untrodden spaces
arid like stellar surfaces where you
have lived for long and you are met
again by faceless hooded shapes that
creep in as soon as heaven's troops
are gone, or where they have not yet been?
—those shades of drabness, lingering traces
of early agonies that also live in you
but in perennial webs of mist,
the hurts that claim their origin
far back in the ancestral birth...
'Reclaim, react, rebel, defy! flesh that
you are and you need not, cannot deny!'
Like snails to moss on walls, clinging
to loss, dissatisfactions, lead you
to heightened fantasies, acts that
do not abolish, as they suggest,
but only strengthen them, who claim
and have this hold on you by this,
that you are human because of them.
Any reprieve into the glare
of heaven's light where they
must fall apart like ash, enrages them
—like wasps that strike though they
must die—to monstrous irritations.

8.

It is not they who make me what I am,
those hordes freed all around me, freed since
the images that had controlled them fell
and people turning from their hold on them
made room for grievances long hidden and
denied, the darknesses in them too long
ignored, the hurts too long repressed.
Now they occupy the sad terrain strewn with
the broken imagery, pieces of noble heads,
rumps of horses misshapen into the dial
of time, the rummage of idols and of dreams
the sole possessors of the sunset scene.
A death announced but not an heir. They are
the furies who, once freed, release themselves
in each. As they have done in me,
who, for a while rebellious at a
rebellious age, took up their cause.
But recognized them as the source of
misery and, struggling for distance, broke
their hold on me. For it is the destructive force
they serve, discontinuity, ego-
centricity, the never ceasing demands
of the disgruntled self, prodigal, expelled.
Once seen for what they are they change
their guise, proclaim themselves on heaven's
side, that it is they, the acts they indicate
which are our means toward it, though all
the while, insidiously, feeding the doubt
—which sense proves it?—that it exists.
Chameleon-like, lecherous for nothing
but to survive, arch-enemy of man,
it is not they who make me what I am.

9.

But what they oppose, that stands fixed,
compassionless in their regard,
opposing them, has made me what I am
far back as I recall. In earliest
sights of luminous distances,
of hills and waters, slopes of vine,
of ample lawns and darknesses of trees
in parks full of a lingering pomp
of time, of silences, of broken or-
naments, of stone; in faces, later on,
a comprehension caught in eyes
so full it cannot be said, of loss,
of hopes, of possibilities—young in-
timations of supreme acknowledgment
expressed as love, and of its pain;
for nothing lasts in this, our human realm,
the eyes, the slender hands confessed.
And mostly, that I looked even then
before I knew what suffering was
upon a suffering face with pity—
for a mother's inability to change
the course of things, reverse a fate,
or as a boy for a friend whose boyish limbs
as he stood, arms crossed, near where
I sat, spoke to me first of
the fragility of our lives.
From where, that early on, the need
to give assurance, and of what?
To say to someone struggling with
a loss, divesting himself as though
digging frantically, of the life
that has kept him apart, the outerwear,
the piles of paper he doesn't want,
to be close again to the secret intact,
the substance, the salve of the gods:

that it is there, from where we've come,
that all along it has been undisturbed,
that it cannot be reached as place,
which never disappears as it does not
appear, there where our home resides,
the gleam we here perceive belongs,
the unseen throbbing like air following
a burst of bells...

10.

They come, also in dreams, the mistakes
of every age, wander about in the vast
mist-held fields of their regret, figures
whose minds are gone, who cannot weep,
who come to us that we may weep for them,
so they may fade, by retracing far as
we can, by digging out from our memory
the cause that caused the error to begin—
o error, error that must plague us
the more that heaven's shine, some com-
prehension of the origin brings into view
the mists wherein they must remain encased,
the torments that may fade but never quite
dissolve, o disconsolate figures
that are to us what misshapen forms
must be to those who brought them forth,
whom they must pity if not love,
or love the more for their complicity
in the emergence of distorted lives.
Nor is it just in dreams where this
disturbance lies. The causes of
disharmony being so many and so old,
to be rid of the great roar of their demand,
the power in the blood, have we
not done, have I not done, as they
would have us do? But the great, the patient source
in us is merciful. It is not asked
that we do any more than we can do.
It is not asked that we be killed by their
attack. Only that we do not favor them.
That we battle, but not be on their side.

11.

There will be moments, and they have already been,
you may be aware that they have,
or that they eluded you
as the brightness of certainty,
of knowledge does when we wake,
the times when the person you are,
the desires that have both shaped and unsettled you,
longings and errors borne by the very stones,
the very cloth of the setting
into which you came, walks, rooms,
tall squares dark as sleep,
amongst which you have moved and move,
also at the end of passages
sudden views of spaces bright as sun,
an ocean before you or a descent
of valleys, flowers, flowers,
field after golden field turning into distance
and a blue arising, unearthly, ethereal...

There will be moments
when all that the past has made you,
that is present within you,
has sunk to the ground, lying there
passive, humble like initiates
their foreheads touching the floor
deferring to a greater force, the greater force;
or, like a master's hounds sitting,
their paws stretched before them,
seemingly listening to the master speaking on his return...

There will be moments
when you are not there,
when your terrors, hopes, even your secrets
lie obedient as though non-existent,
and there takes hold of you

the greater force that also exists in you,
and it takes hold of you
like the dance of the dancer,
the creator of what he has created

and as you lift up your leg
in the dance of his dance,
as you lift up your arm
in the reach of his hold,
as you hold up your head
in the pose of his might
and as there falls from your eyes
the joy of his joy

there is then nothing but
the shimmer of his shimmering being,
his shimmering vastness and
the shimmering sounds,
the trembling sounds of his joy...

and the earth is his shimmer,
the fields, the trees and the stones,
and the water and the sky
his shimmering flow that
has never never been
anything else, never anything
but what it is...

and you let it happen, it has become
itself in you, and you do not
hold on to it, you let it be,
you must let it be, you do not try
to have it happen again,
you did not bring it about

you only let it be
you let it be
that which was you
that which is you
and is gone

12.

There is only this that you must do
if the cry in the depth of your being
heard by you in the best of dreams,
by others seen in the far-away look
like the language of yearning in your eyes;
if—other gratifications notwithstanding,
acts of the body the body demands,
forgetfulness and the reach into
the taste of the timeless, the place, limbs of
the gods, the body can accomplish—
if your deepest, your relentless desire
is for unceasing closeness to
the precincts, even the outermost stretches,
watery borders, lights reflected and swaying
as in lagoons around the canal-crossed city;
if what you want ultimately is to be near always
to at least the furthermost reaches of heaven.
There are, on earth, places, not only fortresses, cities
but coasts blue as bright midnight, inlets, coves
blending the gentle aspects of water and land,
of colors, of homes, of gardens, and there
are fields and there are streets and squares
and tree-bordered lawns and ponds which suit
the hidden aspect, the grandiose but gentle concept
that is the hidden world of heaven,
are appropriate to, approximate its nature,
are the visible expressions of its invisibleness.
There have been men and women, men and women
who when immersed entirely in heaven within,
when absorbed by it looked upon their earth,
cancelling thereby the demarcations, making
of what is within without, and without within;
their look, that look cast then, the instant of
this merging upon the earth—having thus
transformed the land, its essence expressed,

heaven's contours brought forth—lasts still.
So you must try to stand. In harmonious
relation to the invisible in you
which only your reception of the given world,
your acts, gestures, looks, words can
make visible. And do not ask that it
possess you, that it break through in you,
becoming itself in you, as once,
or perhaps more than once, it did.

13.

A drive to Pontlevoy, past fields
of heather, of corn, past sunflowers tall
as wheat, each in the vast field turned
as in one huge obedience, toward the sun.
How many drives have there not been,
at midday, or sunset when
the flowers have turned the other way,
to visit friends, meet trains, or just see
the countryside, walk through towns.
How many places have we not seen
that are nowhere now but in reflections,
like the entire ascending side of a town on a hill
in the wide river we drove along
on our way back in the evening, all that had seemed
solid, the trees, lampposts, old walls,
nothing but the watery flow
we possess in the end. The sixteenth-century
abbey, the Sun-king's symbol in stone
above the door where the Dauphin had slept—
added impressions in a stream of
impressions, of pomp
once real, of facades once decorated
for arrival or a death. Only
the look, and no matter how many, there is
only one, only the look that receives,
has received that which is actual,
only the look remains at the end of day.
Appearances, not as fixed and solid
but as flowing, as reflected in
the wateriness of time, as contained
forever in the river that flows
nowhere, that is the view of heaven.

14.

For us, nonetheless, irrevocable departures,
always the loss. And of that other denial
far more wounding than the illusion of
appearances, than the betrayal of time?
That it cannot be had on earth,
too many examples are told of it,
the beloved beyond human measure,
the beloved, fleeing, caught forever as a tree;
nations warring because of one man's reach
for the love beyond man's power to possess;
a youth tricked by poisons from attainment,
his desperate schemes to make permanent
what he had glimpsed, had had, of bliss,
but fleetingly; another man's rage, revenge
in murder when the love he had possessed
was ruined by another's envy and deceit:
none of it can last, can be made to be
possessed, heaven's hidden lineaments,
heaven's bliss the body has.
And for those who must reach that far,
who are not content unless they have found
in another, in a burst, an illumination,
the features they have sensed in themselves,
their most cherished, hidden visage
in the total person, pose of nothing but
perfection, in the other, in the other's arms;—
for those who are not complete, and they
have always been among us, who cannot cease
to quest for the very reach that has made them,
are not complete unless in one touch
they have touched and been touched by
what is behind each creature, uniting all:
for those who cannot cease unless they
have thus been loved, and love—how do
they live with this injunction, that henceforth,

though their desires do not die, their
demands must cease? That it must be enough,
times passing, the passing images of love!
That it cannot be made their own, cannot
be brought into their realm, that they
must let it fade from them, dissolve—
the body of perfection they have seen,
a descent of heaven standing in the river,
perfection in the body standing in the water,
in a gathering distance, a gaining haze.

15.

Invariably, having been close to the courts
that aroused the awareness of heaven in me,
of harmonies, scenes mine once and now
vibrant again, that brought them to life
again, in actualities, in dreams;—
far away places, the silhouette of him
who lifted my being up, who swept by,
a white cloth over his shoulder, almost like
a being of air, almost as though he weren't there,
leaving a trail of blue, remembrance
of love hurt, young love hurt, restored,
a bloom of deliverance in my eyes,
the child's hand in his mother's, the world
well again, innocence real once more. . .
Or walking in streets, squares, towns,
the countryside around them as artful as
the art it produced, of harmonious
perspectives, of the lady of modest demeanor;
or in dreams when I found again a brother's
love, and there exists between us a oneness
as in the looks of those bound by
the same love, the love for him in whom
it is incarnate, and it is in the dream
engaging, fulfilling, heightened, amorous,
the love in brothers for one another
and for the love that is the same in them. . .
Invariably, there follows then
a rousing of old wants stirring the body's
irritants, an urge that would lead to acts,
to scenes that can well be imagined—
the opposite of the courts of benevolence,
of the gracious bestowing of love,
the settings, details of the blood's rage
having been depicted, recounted often enough.
Invariably then, let it be said,

loss and longing for his benevolence
having made one find one's way back,
he is there on one's return, unchanged,
attentive as though awaiting one,
the fullness overflowing, overwhelming,
for who but he knows the conflict he causes
—indifferent, implacable, immovable?

16.

Since the solid, indicated world
is only seemingly so, appearances
vanishing as if dreamed, the slopes,
uphill, downhill, scenes we look at
longingly, of shady gardens, roofs,
of cattle sitting, horses drinking at ponds,
of rolling hills whose gentle aspects
caress us as we pass them giving us
the restfulness, blessed assurance
we seek, deprived of them—of a soil
so drenched— in someone's arms; since these
and other scenes we live with, have lived with,
occurrences long ago, whole ages recorded,
their achievements viewed now as ruins,
as remnants, as grand, often extravagant
displays on walls; since whole ages gone
and the years of our lives we remember,
scene after scene of the solid world
dissolve, rise up to us as dreams, live on
as our remembrance, often our torments,
secrets that have to be released or it
is killed in us, our ease with it, with this
their continuance, reception:
Since even the expressions in the body,
the realization in human form of
the stature that belongs to nothing but
permanence, immanent, invisible,
is for us always shrouded in distance,
perfection glimpsed but never owned,
heaven's look looked at that will hound us
as only beauty in the body can,
will run, all our lives, through our days:
—Since nothing that yields itself
to our perception is solid, permanent,
what of that that lures us on, that is

not caught in its appearances? Is it not
in us? Does it not hide in us
without whom appearances would not
appear, would not record, reflect
themselves, their splendor not resonate,
perfection not be recognized,
the ideal they possess, remembered?

17.

He rules there, is not hidden, lives,
nearer than nearness, as though hidden,
in the depth of our being, hangs on our eyes
just as we wake, just as we look upon
his form in the first form before us,
the shape that has risen in our eyes,
space and time having become the shape
that has risen to be recognized,
that has risen to be received.

He rules there to where each returns.
Out of him, in us, the splendor we look at
on hills, the sights now wasted;
out of him, in us, the love in the eyes,
the light in quickness in the face
before us, in the hand ours moves toward;
out of him, in us, the complete body
standing before us, the sky as backdrop;
out of him, in us, the perfect body
standing at a distance in the water;
out of him, in us, the harmony
as we sit near a lamp, our eyes closed;
out of him, in us, the music
of farewell, of hopes for a safe journey,

the music we hear in the dark,
in a dark square in our sleep,
that speaks of the heart, consoles and consoles...
out of him, out of him
on our eyes, our depth,
the secret dissolved,
the secret cleared as we wake...

the years are gone, the ages
but he hangs on our eyes as we wake
and is the same

18.

For days I've been as in a blissful slumber
although the impressions of things around me
have never been more vivid, of the four poplars
taller than pillars at ancient sites, their tops swaying, rustling;
of the hill beyond, or of the massive stone supports
where the bridge starts that leads a canal across, above the river
on whose bank we walked, sometimes wading through puddles
left by the river or by yesterday's storm. Although I've been
as in a daze, the reception by an invisible flow, firm essence of
my being, firmer, no doubt, than the stone supports
or the roots permitting the giant treetrunks to sway
as in a steady rhythmic ritual, solemn dance,
—the reception of details never more vivid
has never, unless in a dream, or on occasions
so rare only the wholeness can be remembered,
the details a blur: has never, or rarely been
as unimpeded, as immediate, the impressions
seeming to become at once the air that held them
and the invisible essence, depth that received them.

And as I listened during these days to some of the great works
the composers of two, three centuries ago have left us,
and even of those more recent who struggled still
and in the end succeeded to find again and state again
a faith, a purpose, a redemption (one such work engaging
a thousand instruments and voices), I felt that it had all come
        together,
all that can be said, demonstrated of value, demolishing
every notion so that the one thing, one essence, only fact,
fixed fact that moves us, can be revealed, can be allowed
to be itself...

And I thought, almost hearing it said, that the masters have said so,
it has all come together... the compassion, the structure

—no sound, no language, no form
giving music its sound, language its strength, form its purpose—
invisibleness giving myriad shapes, myriad constellations,
                              form, grandeur, flow...

it has all come together...in utterance, in the look,
the caring look upon the supplicant, the caring look
upon the soil like hands lifted in blessing

it has all come together...at the source of utterance,
where the needy, the restless dead, the spirit neglected
in living things, gather timidly in the rose-light of evening
                              in the shadow of palms...

And I thought, the masters have said so, in music,
in intimations, in silence: it has all come together
in him, in him who has walked, invisibly, yet visible,
who is always the same, the changes equal at his eyes,
who walks and will walk, freeing at each step
the delightful being on his shoulder, giving back
to air what is air, to spirit what is spirit,
making us aware at each step, at each step making us know
the miracle, one miracle, the unknowable, unperceivable,
                              constant and forever.

And I thought: As I am, and know that I am,
as I am sublimely awake, adrift in this blissful slumber,
why would I doubt? And I looked at the poplars,
at the wind deep in their branches,

at the evidence of wind deep in their branches,
and I looked at the bird and heard it pecking on the wire whereon
      it sat,
and I looked at the dove, the grey mourning dove flying off
its perch below the roof across, making its mournful sound;
and I looked at the stones of the wall where I had put my hand,
and I looked at the vines, and when I got up and walked,

at the fields, rolling fields stretching far into the distance,
and at the trees, dense trees bordering them,
and at the child running before me: and they do not doubt,
do not doubt that they are.
                              And voices came to me, chords,
voices in chorus, and from one of the masters, the most lyrical,
shattering song on the clarinet, from out of my sleep, the bliss
in dreams, the bliss awake

                              * * *

By the water, by the wide river,
below its bank on the stones
where the river has receded,
by the water and the small islet
the river makes, stretches of sand
where the child, naked, plays,
the father stands in the water fishing
and the mother lies in a chair sunning;
by the water, seeing the family,
looking at the trees on the bank across,
at the width of the river, its changing shape,
at the islets, sandy, stony, some
with clusters of bushes, some with trees,
—looking at the river, end to end,
its forms, its borders of stones, of trees
some with roots exposed like veins of mud,
and looking up at the vastness—
above the enormous range the river makes,
the width of its bed and higher, its valley—
stretching, vaulting above all
the sky's deep blue streaked in parts
by trailing threads, or scarfs, of leisurely clouds;
—by the water, by the wide river
the unencompassable height hovering there
like a being, all of it, sky and water,
width and length, child and fisherman,
and over there, a dog wagging its tail
for a stick to retrieve from the water,

all of it, all of it become like a being,
one unencompassable, unimaginable yet almost tangible
being, whose presence runs through me,
whose presence breaks through me
to thrills beyond feeling except that I know,
that I know I am moved beyond feeling
and that I am one with, encompassed by
as each thing, each living thing, each element around me
is, all of us held in the oneness of the being
that is there, is actually there, in and
beyond us, holding us, the creator the created,
the essence hovering, I can feel it hovering,
the essence blessing, loving, enjoying what it is

(Châtillon-sur-Loire)

On Another Departure, Châtillon 1987

When silence enters and past times
are recollected as though a lens
had caught beloved images restored
to a brilliant sharpness they may or
may not have had when first perceived,
their look of timelessness down lanes
behind an ornate iron gate slightly ajar;
when such images of moments of former
happiness come back, of people and places,
the ease and oneness between them,
a walk, arm in arm, across a bridge;
among trees dimly lit by lamplight
the tentative urgings of desire:
the longing these arouse in us is not so much
for what actually happened as for
the promise they held, the sweet
anticipation as they occurred.
Years had to have taught us that of our ardent wishes
little has become real; of the beloved visage,
although appearing before us, there has been
no lasting possession. Ultimately, the perfection
of which we receive glimmering impressions
around houses, canals, faces looking up
at our approaching shadows, exists,
continues in its impenetrable realm,
its own glory of constant presence,
for us out of reach except that we
perceive, except that we may feel it. Reminded
of moments charged with its promise,
we continue to look longingly toward
the gate to forgetfulness where at last
we shall be at home, absorbed in
the quiet splendor of its wholeness.

Two

Old Offense

It seems to me in retrospect
I held you as a charioteer
maneuvering his reins holds
the road flying past his wheels,
or as a youth cradling a fawn
lured to his moonlit lawn.
But I was neither racing toward
a shore in antiquity
nor trapping animals to appease
an adolescent's lust.
Another ancient hunger drove me
to seek you out where you, like I,
had come to find more than a
reflection in a stream,
though as capture no more solid in
the end. For, the instant that
you glimpse in someone else's
features a vision of yourself,
familiar but so far back
it does not come up before you
in a mirror, sight blurs,
the injured moment runs,
the flesh in your arms turns
from watery shimmer to stony
stare: and you let go
the damp head in your hands
as if you had transgressed,
had relived an old offense.

Spirit's Taunt

You will not see me
unless you dare storm the body,
break down frontiers and enter
where all sorts of injunctions
tell you you must not.
Forts have been put up
for more than territorial defense.
Shy the face peering out
behind a latticed window.
A box within a box within
a box within many more
holds the piercing treasure.
Behind walls deep in
the central courtyard
blooms the mysterious flower
the color of flesh.
Only from there will you
hear me, see me, will you have
the consolation that I am.
But that is all. I will
cover my face, will pierce
and blank you out if
once there you will try
to take what is not yours—
will think you may remain because
you have dared storm walls
forbidden you by laws.

Dianabad, Vienna 1937

From the wintry sky, clouds august as
slabs of polished stone in crypts,
from the wintry streets, the snow-
covered benches, statues, trees;
from the wintry city into
the steamy bath, his first time at
the *Dianabad,* the renowned place,
with the other boys of his class.

From museum rooms, stone poses,
bronze horsemen and bronze flags;
from formal parks, classrooms,
correct behavior and other
European formalities, to
the steam, the pool, the artificial waves,
the showers and the nakedness.

Was what he had sensed as
locked within canvasses, casts,
faces he had passed in parks, in streets;
was what had seemed to him
buried behind façades
to be freed and touched as
glistening wet nakedness?

Would clouds, all exteriors, distant, cold,
monuments whose indifference
had been both lure and awe to him,
turn into the sheen of flesh?
Can what is desired become close?
And will it be held the way eagles
having broken from stone-like clouds
carry their prey aloft in claws?
How this had baffled him, naked
among naked bodies in the steam!

Dark Converse

Like a block of ancient stone,
mausoleum slab or one that marks
the spot where the oracle sat,
a deep, inexplicable darkness sits,
too habitual to be dissolved, more of
a riddle after all these years.
And when it flares up, flares up
as hurt that cannot be righted,
desire that cannot be quenched.

The dark converse this
of another indication equally
unbroken, of radiance that
on many occasions has flowed
across a face, down a body like sun
in a room on a torso of stone.

Signals

It is not a permanence they seek
(that can be permanent only for
a limited time), it is the fleeting
wherein alone the permanence
that is not limited can shine:
other-than-human beings in human form,
perfect limbs that grow out of
clouds, out of mists, then walk alongside
on dusty roads they took, angels
who impart messages, then leave.

They who seek are in the audience,
have come for nothing less than
a great event, a dancer who in a leap,
a turn can outdo the pulls that hold
others in place; or to hear a pianist
who in a chord, a phrase brings back
the look each has met at one time,
the face that time does not erase.
Or they're in a bedroom seated at
the edge of the bed, rid of

their clothes, about to embrace
the person in whom may ascend
the figure both yearn to apprehend;
about to rediscover in private,
in secret, the known, the beloved,
the quintessentially familiar—
for whom, when the signals are there,
they will have come; for whom,
for however brief a time, they will
have left their ordinary lives.

Antibes, The Evening Hours

When a paleness the color of slumber
covers the land just before night falls
and the small birds whose feathers had
shimmered like mother-of-pearl, high in
their nests are heard no more, people
not protected by ties or by routine—
migrant workers when their work is done,
tourists when museums close; fierce-eyed
Algerians, bewildered young Americans
and others unattached—stand along
the stone wall that runs along the coast.
Far from home and feeling lost when
the vast blandness of hushed light
descends, distinctiveness all blotted out,
no murmurings from the sleep in trees,
they are soothed somehow—facing the sea's
       unmatched prominence, its
       turbulence against the stones.

Outside Gien

Roses in a patch of sun
against stone walls in villages I drive through,
or bursts of wild rose bushes in
the muddy flats just ahead of
the river; roses caught as at
their peak, a clarity so distinct
only their shades stand out,
the details overwhelmed by
the shine of the whole, a trembling
in sunlight of the thing fulfilled:
do they demonstrate in a glimmer
not themselves but the root beyond
division, essence that will break into
rose-colors, into scents, into
spectacles of our pleasure;
—do they bestow on us this rush of
illumination because they will
be gone so soon? Just then,
at that instant in the sun,
do they not represent to us
what we have lost, where we run from,
must run from trapped by time?
Why else do I feel, seeing them
and behind them their somewhat swaying shadows,
as if, having slipped from my world
and having descended far below
the clamors of ejected figures,
images of my own division that must
still haunt my bed: —why else do I feel just then
as if the wholeness of roses in the sun
had put me back in the state I'm in
neither awake nor dreaming?

77th Street Fair

As usual, from the moment I wake
and adjust myself to where I am,
(as in a lens the right distance is found
by adjustment so that images appear
in focus, and a rider gallops across
at proper speed and atop the mountains
marksmen observe him through a lens on
their guns)—as usual, as day
proceeds I am aware of absence.

Sunday. I walk down a sunny street.
A fair is going on. Stands
for food and merchandise; a caravan
of baby-carriages occupied and led
by ribboned Persian cats; a handful
of onlookers, some with fine, delicate
faces, stand around a young man playing
a Bach aria on the flute: "I am
not lost" it says, *I am not lost!*

Around the corner the crowd disbands.
There is the whine of emptiness
as of projectiles whizzing past.
I spot a figure up ahead.
Adjusting myself to this possibility—
your presence in the empty street—
I find, after all, it is not
your shape that's there, only its space,
its space like a cutout of emptiness
ablaze in windless air.

Mozartian

I must not let it get away,
the song I dreamed I sang,
Mozartian tunes of an
assuredness only one
element that sings through us
is capable of. It surrounded me
as I lay in the dark, return
not loss of those we loved with
our changeless selves, the un-
demanding love the song
conveyed; —flickers of
this shadow upon the dream's
tall squares, old stones,
stayed on into the day.

Now, under a wintry sky,
along the highway and amid
a stream of cars—on a sparse lawn
a man huddled in his coat
impatient for his dog
to stop sniffing and be done—
now as I talk to the others,
and we can only reach so far
(irritations mostly),
I turn when nothing is said
to be sure that it is there,
to listen for it, to hear
far far back in the dark
its unchanged song, its unchanged lilt.

To Daniel, A Student

You are keenly aware still
of differences: between the things
that fade and wind that takes
the layers as they peel but
surrounds, sustains as well
plantings as they break toward air.

Understand still the difference
between the seed, the tree, the child
that like them grows, things that
can reach to prominent heights
spotted by stragglers from afar,
growth that can break into words,

into songs stirring those
who are stealing close—
uphill through bushes, brambles—
to high thoughts, giving them
what they need most: expansion,
the dark breaking into burnished gold.

Understand still that you cannot blame
decay of things on air that
unchanging, sustains, surrounds them.
Bemoan, alone, out in your boat, the heron
pierced above a blackened coast,
the disappearance as you think of it

of leaves on walls, the length of day
as autumn goes; —but do not resent,
let yourself be comforted by wind;
your hands, your hair-blown face
by currents as they rise,
by distances that do not pass you by.

Art Songs, or, Crossovers

"...It is he, anew, in a freshened youth
And it is he in the substance of his region..."
—Wallace Stevens

1.

Reminiscent of scenes—of shapes,
of formlessness, one and distinct,
of crossovers—the songs now heard
and others these bring back,
and of what now as ever from
its own capacity is figured forth:
the human beauty incomparable at
the crossover-point, reclined
or standing up as if to pose—
for hearts, astonished, passed—
and always, be it on rocks, a
platform or a bed, moving
from out of mists back into mists,
on azure seas, in sunset dreams.

2.

Crossovers. The god into stalks
of rye trembling, into doorposts
—across dark ceilings unseen clouds—
into thighs benumbed, as ice into water
melting as flesh in a dream.
Men, women, crossing over,
crossing over, in and out.
This urge, to mingle with
material, combine into invisibleness,
an unmistakable presence felt,
this flame that comes to each,
each at some time, not
tended, not understood,
unjoined, dies down.

3.

Not accomplishable where
the visage of its gentle features
—across lawns amid trees in bloom,
along coasts in bright haze of foams—
is unapprehended, unattended,
out of focus even in eyes
seeking what the heart knows
but arms have not yet held,
only in dreams, windows open,
the bed long, the scene's bodies,
colors never again forgotten,
the ineffable realized,
sea-eyes, sea-face at
the land's disappearance.

4.

As if a harp or lyre on view,
your limbs spoke of your body's needs
which, of the spirit, you can't
envision in appropriate terms.
That perfected bodies painted on ceilings
swirl cloud-like out of reach,
that truly desiring eyes
are upward, inward turned,
thorns dug forever in the skin:
you have sought to reverse this,
to shape the unattainable to your demands.
But, time and again, the grip loosens,
electric noises stop, darkness and
the sky's first grey return.

5.

A figure, ancient, always young,
walks through the dust, his loose
garments wavering. He is there,
on roads between monasteries, huts,
palatial edifices on peaks,
between dry riverbeds and clouds.
Space and time have concentrated
their vastnesses in him, stars
his eyes, distances his skin.
Death crosses over in his heart.
He is there, ready to be let in,
but you have exiled him,
have kept him from his place
empty and aching within.

6.

Crossovers. Through and into you,
into more than formlessness,
each song received by you,
each time absorbed within
your reservoir of sheerest being.
The gull losing its contours in
the distances of sky and sea,
a burst of wings
out of yourself and dreams.
Only once you are attentive to
essence dissolved back into you,
shall it be the glow wherewith
we shall again perceive
unearthly contours earthly forms contain.

7.

Of nostalgic memories, enough,
of seeing with eyes shut the rooms
where songs as these were heard,
the doors open, rooms filled with
sounds from the fountains below,
the scent of chestnut trees,
muted light of their dense leaves;
enough of remembering the in-
termittent, fragrant silences.
Now let sounds take us back
to the true source of songs
—the body's resplendent reservoir
of sounds' and light's refractions—
these songs are reminiscent of.

8.

Compassionate tones in the quiet
sections, what is the nature of
the understanding and the pain
works of art we turn to contain?
Stirrings that remind us of inveterate
darknesses in us but also that we
are heard, enfolded again as once
we were. And when by instinct in despair
we take a radical inner turn and for
the quickest instant stand steeled
in absolving light, from where
the healing force we assent to, know that we
have known, a cast across the face,
however fleetingly, of blessedness?

9.

Only through him, who goes
to where he comes from, in us,
will the soil take on contours of
the invisible he gives off
as heavenly bodies rays,
as beauty—the harmony supreme
and not adaptable to our human will—
musical airs. Unchanged
the road he takes. Dust only
obscures but has not wiped out
his steadiness. How will
the ineffable be made manifest
but through the flesh,
his physical steadiness?

0.

Who is the same in us, through whom
the one condition beyond strife,
where sameness rules as air
our physical lives, is reached,
stretches of space into endlessness,
mists across lawns on earth,
a haze of foams along coasts,
sky colors on walls and windows where
lovers are observed in dreams.
It is for greater nearness to him
as I go about routines of the day
that I combat my darknesses,
not to stray from facing toward
the background where he always is.

11.

As the stamen in the lily's hood,
he in his cover, the place he never leaves,
from where when he shines, shines forth:
the background that remains unchanged
despite things of this world that hurl
at us their fate, destined as each is,
however much enlarged, to fade,
be shredded, torn, or just forgotten.
Why should I not be tired of
inevitable waste,
this vengeful littleness,
and not be faced toward that
through whom alone we can be one,
O steadiness, in us, love's origin?

12.

To enter by the open window,
a curtain fluttering outside,
to be received as only a god is,
to pour over your body as only light can,
from another room the music,
the singer's art and feelings
in her portrait in the polished wood.
At the crossover-point, though fleetingly,
neither asleep nor quite awake,
see then, see in the shore's
intensest light as if a gull ablaze,
in the subsuming brightness
beyond the routine changes,
our found, joined features shine!